# One-Hour Christmas Crafts for Kids

Cindy Groom Harry® and Staff, Designs & Consultation

PUBLICATIONS INTERNATIONAL, LTD.

W9-AVJ-028

Copyright © 1993 Publications International, Ltd. All rights reserved. This book may not be reproduced or quoted in whole or in part by mimeograph or any other printed or electronic means, or for presentation on radio, television, videotape, or film without written permission from:

Louis Weber, C.E.O.
Publications International, Ltd.
7373 North Cicero Avenue
Lincolnwood, Illinois 60646

Permission is never granted for commercial purposes.

Manufactured in USA.

8 7 6 5 4 3 2 1

ISBN 0-7853-0400-2

Cindy Groom Harry is an author, crafts designer, and industry consultant whose work has been widely published in her own numerous craft books, and through hundreds of articles that have appeared in publications including *Better Homes and Gardens*, *McCall's Needlework and Crafts*, and *Craftworks for the Home*. She is a member of the Society of Craft Designers, where she previously served on the board of directors, and has also taught and demonstrated her designs on television craft programs.

Photography by
Sacco Productions Limited/Chicago

Photographers: Peter Ross, Cindy Trim

Photo Stylist: Missy Sacco

Photo shoot production: Roberta Ellis

Illustrations by Cindy Groom Harry® and Staff, Designs & Consultation

Royal Model Management models: Elizabeth Gonzalez, Mary Beth Johnson, Steven Kriz, Ashley Pincus

The mention of any product is merely a record of the procedure used and does not constitute an endorsement by the respective proprietors of Publications International, Ltd., nor does it constitute an endorsement by any of these companies that their products should be used in the manner recommended by this publication.

## SOURCE OF MATERIALS

The following products were used in this book:
**Aleene's™ Shrink-It Plastic:** 30; **Aleene's™ Tacky Glue:** 6, 10, 14, 24, 30, 34, 38, 41, 48, 51; **Aleene's™ Tack-It Over & Over Glue:** 54; **The Beadery® Beads:** 45; **The Beadery® Gemstones:** 38, 45, 54; **Bedford Bendable™ Ribbon:** 21, 27; **Black & Decker® 2 Temp™ Glue Gun:** 14, 18, 21, 24, 27, 45, 54; **Black & Decker® 2 Temp™ Glue Sticks:** 14, 18, 21, 24, 27, 45, 54; **Cadillac Co. Global Effects Globe:** 18; **Delta Ceramcoat™ Paint:** 10, 30, 41; **Design Master® Color Tool Spray Paint:** 45; **DMC Embroidery Floss:** 6; **Duncan Scribbles® Dimensional Paint:** 10, 18, 48; **Duncan Scribbles® Outline Pen:** 10, 30, 41; **The Felters Co. Craft 100® Felt:** 10, 14, 18, 30, 38, 41, 51, 54; **Fiskars® For Kids:** 6, 10, 14, 18, 21, 27, 30, 34, 38, 41, 45, 48, 51, 54; **Fiskars® For Kids Craft Snips:** 21; **FloraCraft Blue Jay Chenille:** 14, 18, 21, 27, 41, 45; **FloraCraft Blue Jay Tinsel Stem:** 6; **Forster™ Clothespins:** 41; **Forster™ Toothpicks:** 6; **Hunt Bienfang® Stampable™ Notecards:** 24; **Hunt X-Acto® Pliers:** 41; **Magnetic Specialty, Inc., Magnetic Tape:** 10; **One & Only Creations Original-Curl™, Mini Curl™ Curly Hair™:** 41; **Putnam Co., Inc., Soft Shapes Fiberfill:** 14, 18; **Silver Brush, Ltd., Silverwhite™ Paint Brushes:** 10, 30, 41, 54; **Spinrite Plastic Canvas Yarn:** 10; **Wrights® Rattail Cord:** 30, 34; **Wrights® Ribbon:** 14, 18, 21, 30, 38, 48, 51; **Wrights® Rick Rack:** 30.

# contents

# introduction

## dear parents and teachers—

We know that most kids will be able to make the projects with very little help, but there will be times when your assistance is important. If the child has never used a glue gun, please explain that the nozzle, as well as the freshly applied glue, is warm, even when set on a low temperature. Have a glass of water nearby just in case warm fingers need cooling. Occasionally, instructions direct the child to ask for adult help in a certain place. Be sure everyone understands the "Important Things to Know" section on the facing page. The general directions concerning patterns contain important instruction, too.

Above all, we want to emphasize that this should be an enjoyable, creative experience. Although we provide very specific instructions, it's wonderful to see children create their own versions, using their own ideas. ENJOY!

## hey kids—

Christmas is a very special time of year. With *One-Hour Christmas Crafts for Kids,* you can make the season even merrier! This book will show you how to make terrific trimmings for the tree, dynamite decorations for your home, cool cards to send, and pleasing presents to give to family and friends. There is something for everyone in this book!

*One-Hour Christmas Crafts for Kids* was made with you in mind. Many of the projects are fun things you can make by yourself. However, sometimes you will be instructed to ask for help from an adult.

It's a good idea to make a project following the written instructions exactly. Once you understand how to do it, feel free to make it different the next time. You might want to change the color of the paint or floss. There are many ways you can personalize each project to add a special touch. Think of all the variations you can make and all the gifts you can give!

Most important, HAVE FUN! Just think how proud you'll be to say, "I made this!"

## key:

Each project has been tested to measure the challenge level it presents to the crafter. The chart below shows you the key to the levels. Look for these stars above the title of each project.

easy                    medium

challenging

## general pattern instructions

When individual project instructions direct you to cut out a shape according to the pattern, begin by tracing the pattern from the book onto typing paper, using a pencil. If the pattern has an arrow with the word FOLD next to a line, it is a half pattern. Fold a sheet of typing paper in half, then open up the paper. Place the fold line of the typing paper exactly on top of the fold line of the pattern, and trace the pattern. Then refold and cut along the traced line, going through both layers of paper. Open for the full pattern.

To attach a pattern to felt, roll 2-inch lengths of masking tape into circles with the adhesive side out. Attach the tape to the back of the pattern in several places. Place the pattern onto the felt, and cut through both the paper and felt layers along the lines. If you are using a half pattern, open the pattern and similarly tape it to the felt before cutting.

## important things to know!

Although we know you'll want to get started right away, please read these few basic steps before beginning:

**1.** Go through the book and decide what project you want to make first. Read the materials list and the instructions completely.

**2.** Gather all your materials, remembering to ask permission! If you need to purchase materials, take along your book or make a shopping list so that you know exactly what you need.

**3.** Prepare your work area ahead of time. Clean-up will be easier if you prepare first!

**4.** Be sure that an adult is nearby to offer help if you need it.

**5.** Be careful not to put any materials near your mouth. Watch out for small items, like beads, around little kids and pets.

**6.** Use the glue gun set on the low temperature setting. Do not touch the nozzle or freshly applied glue, because it may still be hot. Use it only with adult permission.

**7.** Always wear an apron when painting with acrylic paints, because after the paint dries, it is permanent. If you do get it on your clothes, wash with soap and warm water immediately.

**8.** When the instructions direct you to paint two coats of a color, let the first coat dry before painting the second.

**9.** Clean up afterwards, and put away all materials and tools.

Take a minute to look at the pictures below. In the materials section for each project, you will find pictures of these frequently used items in addition to the other supplies needed. For example, if you see a picture of a glue bottle, that means you will need thick craft glue to complete that project.

pencil

children's scissors

ruler

glue gun

sandpaper

clear tape

craft snips

thick craft glue

needle-nose pliers

typing paper

water

paper towels

small paint brush     medium paint brush     paper punch

5

# "no worry" angel pin

## materials

Five 2⅝-inch toothpicks
Embroidery floss: white, pink, beige, yellow

10-inch length gold tinsel stem
1½-inch pin back

## instructions

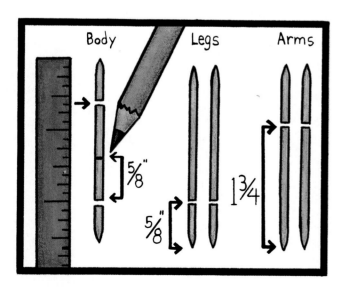

**1.** With help from an adult, cut off and throw away ⅝ inch from each end of one toothpick. Use a pencil to make a mark ⅝ inch from one end. This is the body. Set aside. Use two more toothpicks to make the legs. Cut off and throw away ⅝ inch from one end of each. For the arms, use the remaining two toothpicks. Cut off and throw away 1¾ inches from one end of each.

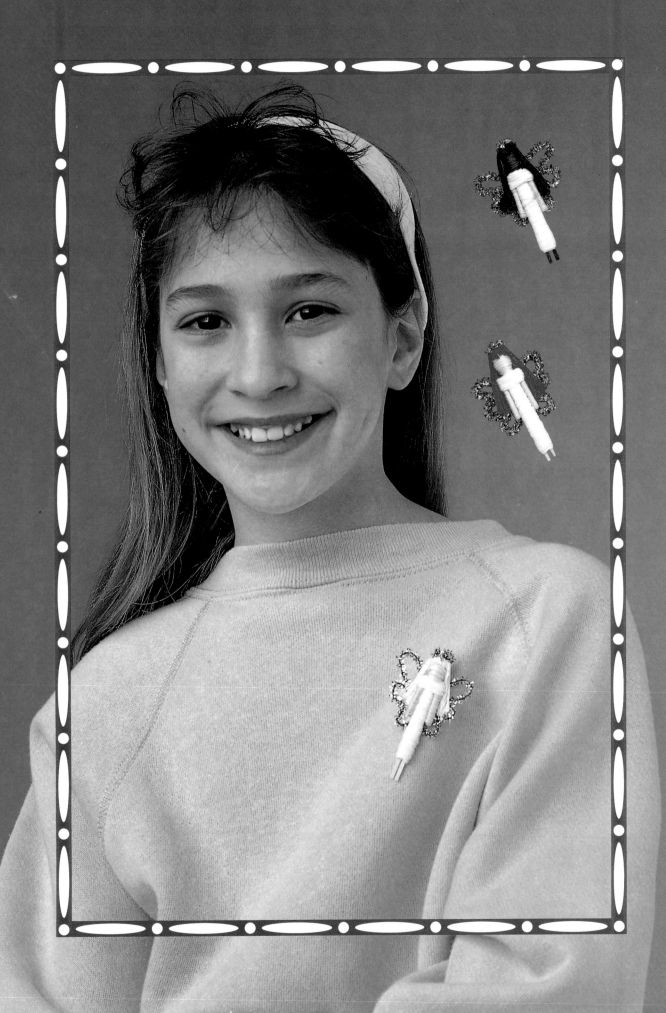

**2.** Glue one leg toothpick to each side of the body, with the pointed ends even with the pencil mark on the body toothpick. Apply a dot of glue to the pencil mark on the body, and place the end of the white floss into the glue. Wrap the floss around the toothpicks, row after row, working your way down. Stop wrapping ½ inch from the end of the legs. Cut the floss, and glue the end in the back.

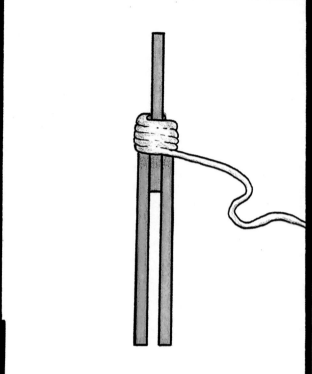

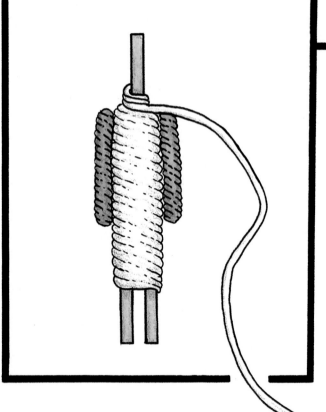

**3.** With the pink floss, use the gluing and wrapping method from Step 2 to completely wrap each arm. Glue the arms to the sides of the body, lining up the top of each with the top of the white floss. To make the shoulders, start wrapping the white floss just above the pencil mark, stopping about ¼ inch below the mark. (It will cover the tops of the arms.) Cut the floss, and glue the end in the back.

**4.** To make the head, wrap beige floss around the top of the body toothpick. Continue making layers, working rows up to the top until the head is approximately ³/₈-inch thick. Cut the floss, and glue the end in the back. For hair, cut eight 4-inch lengths of yellow floss. Align the ends, then fold the lengths in half. Apply glue to the top of the head and place the folded middles in the glue, covering the top and back of the head with floss. Trim hair to the same length all around. Use the trimmed floss to make short bangs and glue in place.

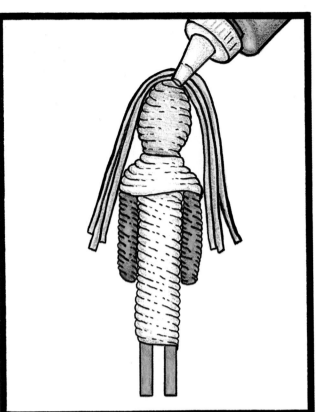

**5.** For the halo, cut a 1-inch length of tinsel stem and wrap it around a pencil. Remove and glue to the top of the head. Use the remaining tinsel stem for the wings. Using the pattern on page 61, bend a 4¹/₂-inch length of the tinsel stem into its wing shape. Repeat for other wing. Glue the wings to the back of the angel. Then glue the pin back to the back of the angel. It's easy to make variations on the angel by simply using a different color of floss and/or painting the legs.

# soldier magnet

## materials

2×6-inch cardboard
Felt: 2×6 inches blue, 2 square inches red, 1×2 inches beige, 1×2 inches black
3-inch length of 2mm gold cord
Dimensional paint: black and glittering gold

1-inch length of ½-inch wide gold braid
Pink acrylic paint
Black fine line felt tip marker
2-inch length black yarn
3-inch length magnetic strip

## instructions

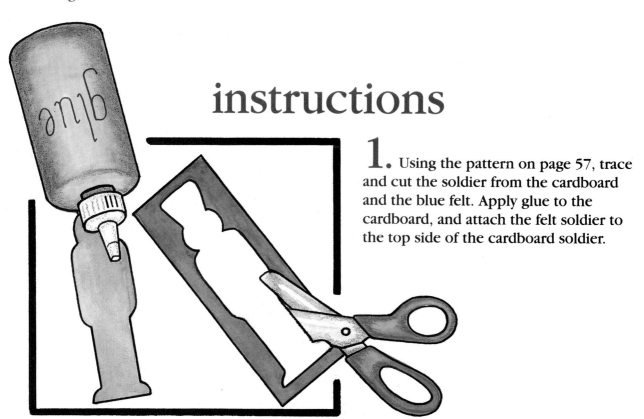

**1.** Using the pattern on page 57, trace and cut the soldier from the cardboard and the blue felt. Apply glue to the cardboard, and attach the felt soldier to the top side of the cardboard soldier.

Christmas List

Mom — Christmas basket a...

Dad — Socks and pine con...

Sis — Tree sweatshirt an...

Nicky — Soldier magnet a...

Misha — Angel pins and s...

Aunt Mary — Candy cane c...

Ms. Brody — teacher Wrea...

* Make cards...

* Finish ornaments f...

**2.** Using the patterns on page 57, trace and cut the jacket from the red felt, the head and hands from the beige felt, and the shoes and cap bill from the black felt. Apply glue to the jacket, hands, head, and shoes. Place these glued pieces into place on the felt soldier. Apply glue to the straight edge of the cap bill, and attach it to the area just above the head.

**3.** Cut eight 3/8-inch lengths of gold cord. Apply glue to two of the cord lengths. Place them on the cap so that they form a "V" shape. Apply glue to three more of the cord lengths. Place these at the bottom of one sleeve. Repeat for the other sleeve. Squeeze paint six gold buttons on the jacket and one large button on the cap at the bottom of the gold cord "V." Let dry.

**4.** Squeeze paint black lines to make the soles of the shoes and to separate the legs and arms. Let dry. Apply glue to a ½-inch length of gold braid, and place it on the jacket shoulder. Repeat for the other shoulder. Paint pink cheeks on the face; let dry.

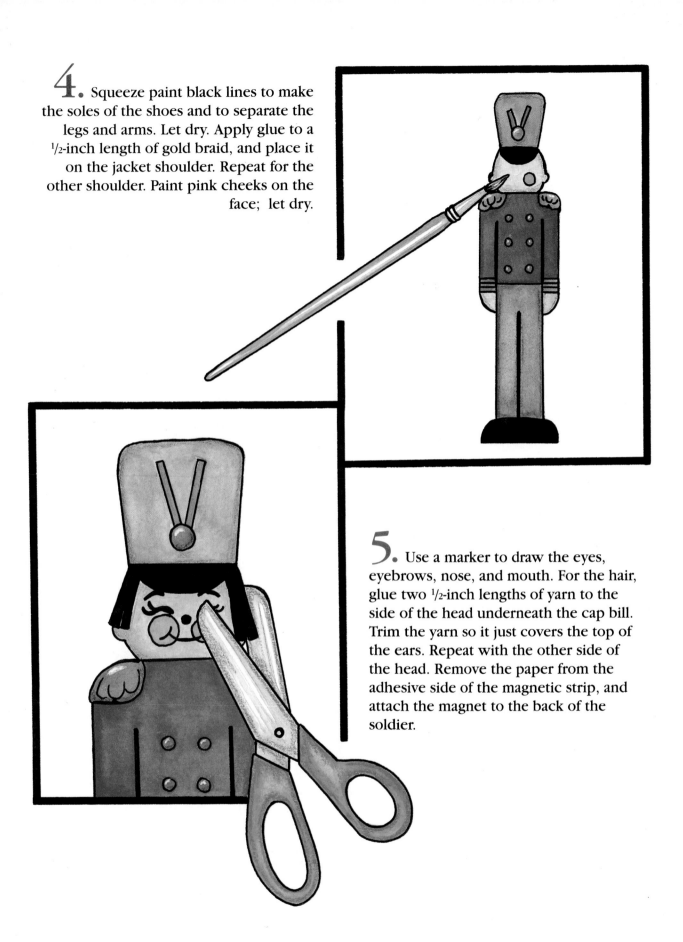

**5.** Use a marker to draw the eyes, eyebrows, nose, and mouth. For the hair, glue two ½-inch lengths of yarn to the side of the head underneath the cap bill. Trim the yarn so it just covers the top of the ears. Repeat with the other side of the head. Remove the paper from the adhesive side of the magnetic strip, and attach the magnet to the back of the soldier.

# santa claus stocking

## materials

Felt: two 9 × 12 inches white,
  one 3 × 4 inches beige, one each
  5-inch and 1-inch squares red
Red satin ribbon: 1-yard 3-inch length
  of ⅝-inch wide, 11-inch length of
  ⅛-inch wide

Small amount fiberfill
Poms: 1-inch white, ¼-inch red
8-inch length white jumbo loopy
  chenille
Two 10mm wiggle eyes
1½-inch length white chenille stem

## instructions

**1.** Using the patterns on pages 58 and 59, trace and cut the stocking foot and cuff from the white felt to make the front. Apply craft glue to the top edge of the stocking. Overlap the top edge of the stocking with the bottom edge of the cuff about ¼ inch. Allow the glue to dry.

**2.** Cut three 6-inch lengths of the ⅝-inch ribbon. Lay the stripes side to side across the cuff, allowing an even amount of white space above, below, and in between each red stripe. (The stripes will be a little bit longer than the cuff. Let the extra length hang over the edge of the cuff for now.) Apply craft glue to the back of each ribbon length, and attach them to the cuff. After the glue has dried, trim the ribbon ends so they are even with the cuff.

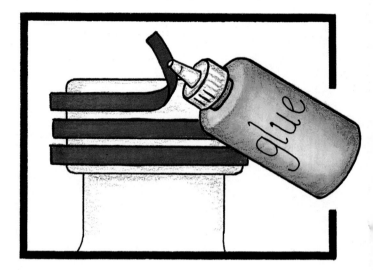

**3.** For the heel, use three 3-inch lengths of the ⅝-inch ribbon. Glue and trim the ribbon as shown on the pattern. Cut a 3-inch length of the ⅛-inch ribbon. Glue it across the top of the heel ribbons to cover the ends. After the glue has dried, trim the ribbon end so it is even with the felt heel. For the toe, cut three 4-inch lengths of the ⅝-inch ribbon. Diagonally position the ribbon on the toe as shown on the pattern. Glue and trim these stripes the same way you did on the cuff.

**4.** Using the patterns on pages 58 and 59, trace and cut another stocking foot and cuff from white felt to make the back. Glue them together as in Step 1, making sure the toe is pointed in the opposite direction. Align the front and back halves, one on top of the other. Lift up the stocking front, and apply a line of glue ⅛ inch in from the edge of the stocking, leaving the top open. Realign the back to the front and let dry. Make the hanger loop by gluing together the ends of an 8-inch length of ⅛-inch ribbon. Insert the ends between the cuff layers on the top right side and glue.

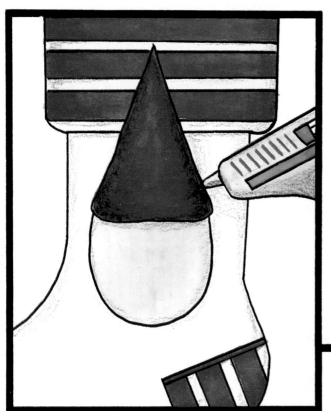

**5.** Using the patterns on page 59, trace and cut the face from the beige felt, the hat and the mouth from the red felt, and the mustache from the white felt. To assemble, use the glue gun. For the hat, roll the red felt into a cone shape, slightly overlapping the straight sides. Glue the overlap area together. Position and glue the top of the face inside the hat. Glue the face and the lower back of the hat to the stocking. Apply glue to the lower front edge of the hat and attach fiberfill. Fold over the tip of the hat and glue to the stocking. Glue a white pom on the tip of the hat.

**6.** For the beard, bend the jumbo loopy chenille into a "C"shape and glue around the face. Glue the red pom nose and wiggle eyes to the center of the face. Glue the mouth and then the mustache onto the face below the nose. For the eyebrows, cut two ³/₄-inch lengths of chenille stem and bend each to curve. Glue above the eyes.

17

# mini-scene ornament

## materials

2½ × 5-inch plastic teardrop globe
White dimensional paint
Poms: one 1½-inch white, two 1-inch
　white, two ¼-inch red
Chenille stem: 6-inch length white,
　1½-inch length green
Felt: ¼ × 6 inches green, 1 square inch
　pink, ½ × 1 inch orange

Two 7mm wiggle eyes
Three 4mm red beads
Small amount fiberfill
⅛-inch wide satin ribbon: 26-inches
　red, 18-inches green
⅝-inch jingle bells: one each red,
　green, white

## instructions

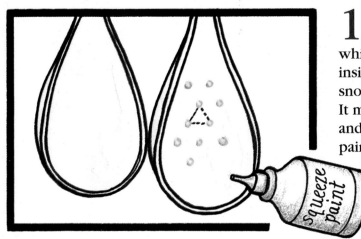

**1.** Separate the globe halves. Using the white dimensional paint, squeeze dots inside each half to give the effect of snow. Space the dots about ½ inch apart. It might be helpful to imagine triangles and place a dot at each point. Let the paint dry.

**2.** To assemble the snowperson, glue the 1½-inch pom (bottom) to a 1-inch pom (middle). Next, glue the other 1-inch pom (head) to top of the middle pom. For the arms, fold in 1½ inches on both ends of a 6-inch length chenille stem. Bend the folded stem into a "C" shape. Glue the inside middle of the "C" shape to the back of the figure.

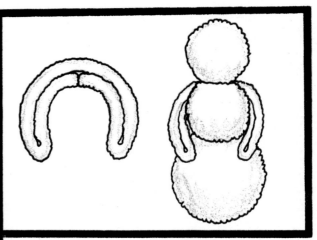

**3.** To make the scarf, angle cut the green felt at both ends. Wrap the middle of the scarf around the neck and tie on one side. Using the patterns on page 61, trace and cut two pink felt cheeks and one orange felt nose. Glue the cheeks to the face just above scarf. Glue the nose to the center of the face between the cheeks. Glue the eyes so that they touch the top inside area of the cheeks. For the earmuffs, bend a 1½-inch length of green chenille into a "C" shape, and glue it to the top of the head. Glue red poms over both ends of the green chenille. Glue three beads down the front.

**4.** Glue a small amount of fiberfill inside the back half of the globe for a snow bank. Glue the finished snowperson on top of the snow. Close the halves. For the bow, cut one 18-inch length of red ribbon and one of green ribbon. Thread two jingle bells onto one ribbon and one jingle bell onto the other. Keeping the bells on the ribbons, insert both ribbons through globe loop. Tie a bow using both ribbons. For a hanger, thread the remaining 8-inch length of red ribbon through the globe loop and knot the ends together.

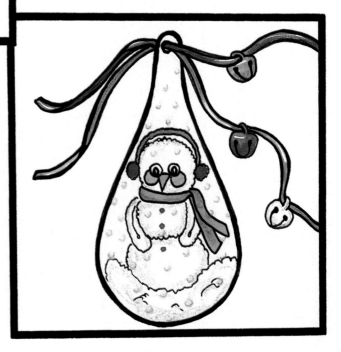

# teacher's wreath

## materials

34-inch length of 1½-inch wide red velvet wired ribbon
34-inch length of 1-inch wide red plaid ribbon
12-inch length red chenille stem
10- to 14-inch greenery wreath
Seven assorted color crayons

6-inch ruler
Small bottle of glue
Pencil
Small scissors
Eraser
Three shiny red plastic apples

## instructions

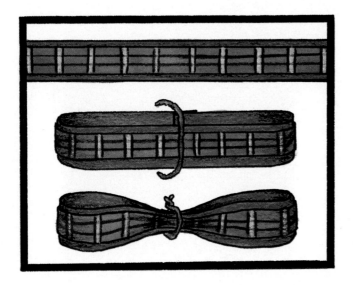

**1.** For the bow, cut an 18-inch length of each ribbon. Position the velvet ribbon horizontally on your work space. After you have aligned the plaid ribbon on the center of the velvet ribbon, glue the ends together. Grasping one end in each hand, fold the ribbon underneath itself, overlapping the ends in the back about 1 inch. Pinch the center of the overlaps together to crimp. To form the two bow loops, cut a 6-inch length of the chenille stem, and wrap it around the crimped middle.

**2.** To make the tails, align and glue the remaining lengths of the ribbons, with the plaid on the top. Pinch the middle to crimp, and position the crimped area under the bow loops. Wrap the chenille stem ends around the center of the tail ribbon; fasten and trim as necessary. Cut a V-notch in the end of each tail ribbon.

**3.** To attach the bow to the wreath, wrap the remaining length of the chenille stem around the middle of the bow. Insert the ends through the branches at the bottom of the wreath. Twist the stem together in the back of the wreath to secure the bow. Trim the chenille ends with the craft snips as needed. Apply glue to two of the crayons, and place them on the middle of the bow to cover the chenille stem binding.

**4.** Arrange the school supplies and apples on the wreath. Once you are happy with the arrangement, glue the supplies into place one at a time.

# cross-stitch-look christmas card

## materials

3 7/8 × 6 inches (42 × 65-squares) white 11-count aida cloth

Fine line fabric markers: gold, red, green

4 3/4 × 7-inch parchment card and envelope

One 5/8-inch gold jingle bell

## instructions

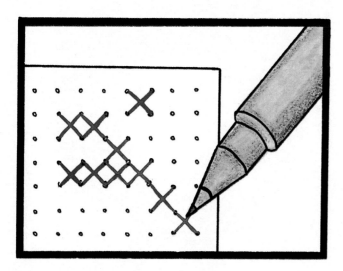

**1.** The distinctive look of cross stitch is usually made with needle and floss on fabric that has a weave made to look like squares. Instead of using a needle and floss, you will use fabric markers to make the X's, carefully drawing from one corner of the square diagonally to the opposite corner. Then make the another line crossing over the first, being careful to draw from corner to corner. Practice making X's on extra aida cloth before beginning this project.

**2.** Following the graph on page 62, and with the help from an adult to get started, make X's on the aida cloth to create a gold bell. Counting the rows of squares (over and down, etc.) on the graph and then on your cloth will help you find your starting place. You'll want to be extra careful not to smudge any of the ink. After the bell is completed, make the red bow and green border.

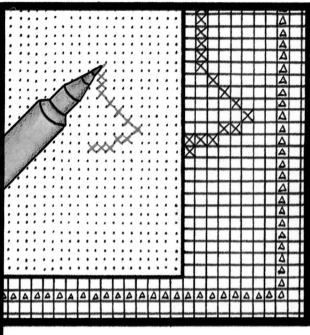

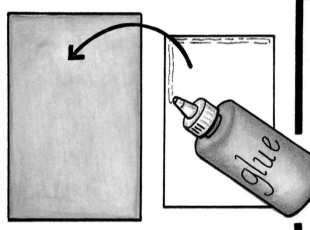

**3.** To mount the aida cloth on the parchment card, apply a thin line of glue along the edges of the back of the aida cloth. Position the cloth on the center front of the card.

**4.** Using the glue gun, place a small amount of glue on the clapper of the bell you have drawn on the cloth. Position the gold jingle bell top-side down in the glue.

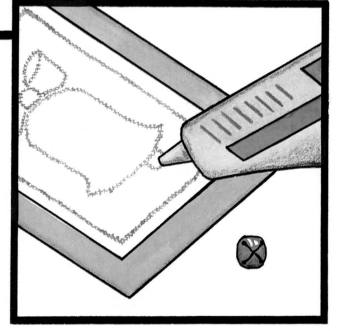

# christmas basket

## materials

Tape measure
Natural raffia basket (9-inch diameter, 10-inch height)
30-inch length of green garland
Red berry picks (approximately thirty-six 9mm berries)

Six ½-inch square miniature gift boxes in Christmas colors
Small amount German statice
34-inch length of 1½-inch wide red velvet wired ribbon
6-inch length red chenille stem

## instructions

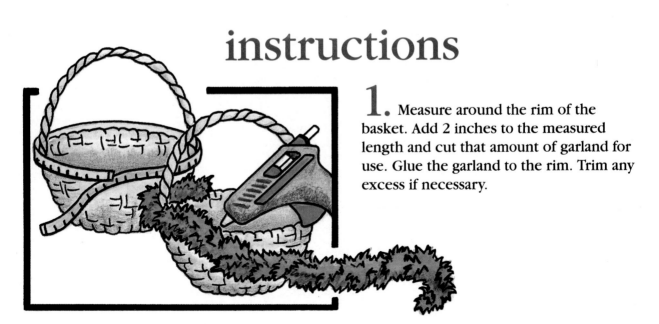

**1.** Measure around the rim of the basket. Add 2 inches to the measured length and cut that amount of garland for use. Glue the garland to the rim. Trim any excess if necessary.

**2.** Cluster the berries into 10 groups: seven groups of three berries and three groups of five berries. Twist the ends of each cluster together. Randomly arrange the clusters in the garland, but do not glue. Arrange the gift boxes in the garland, and then do the same with small sprigs of the German statice. One at a time, remove and glue the berry clusters, gift boxes, and German statice onto the garland.

**3.** To make the bow, cut 30 inches of the red velvet ribbon and bend into thirds, with the ends forming an "X." Pinch the middle together to make the center of the bow. Wrap the 6-inch red chenille stem around the center. Twist the chenille stem ends together at the back to hold, then wrap them around the top center of the basket handle. Bend the ends against the handle. Wrap a 4-inch length of ribbon around the bow center and handle, covering the chenille. Glue the overlapping ends in the back. Cut a V-notch into the ribbon tails.

# gingerbread kid ornaments

## materials

Two 8¼ × 10¾-inch sheets opaque shrink plastic

Black medium point permanent felt tip marker

Pink and brown acrylic paint

Oven and oven mitts

Aluminum foil-covered cookie sheet

34-inch length white baby rick rack

Four 7mm wiggle eyes

1 square inch green felt

Three ⅛-inch red buttons

2-inch length of 1-inch wide green eyelet lace

6-inch length of ⅛-inch wide red satin ribbon

16-inch length of red rattail cord

## instructions

**1.** Read all instructions for shrinking plastic before beginning. Lightly sand both sheets of shrink plastic. Place each sheet on top of the pattern on page 63 and trace with the marker. Remove from the pattern. Paint pink circles for cheeks. Paint the rest with a thin coat of light brown; let dry. Cut out each shape. Punch a hole in each, ½ inch down from the top of the head. To shrink, follow manufacturer's instructions for baking on a foil-covered cookie sheet; cool.

30

**2.** Cut two 14-inch lengths of rick rack. Attach one length around the edges of each shape, applying glue to the back of the rick rack a few inches at a time. Draw a smile and add a dot for the nose with the marker. Glue on the wiggle eyes, keeping them low for a cute look.

**3.** Using the pattern on page 63, trace and cut the tie from the green felt. Glue the tie to the neck of one ornament. Finish this one by gluing three red buttons down the front.

**4.** For the second ornament, begin by gluing lace across the waist. Tie a bow in the ribbon, and glue it to the neck. For hair, glue the center of two 3-inch lengths of rick rack to the top of the head. Be careful not to cover the hole. Spot glue hair at the sides of the head.

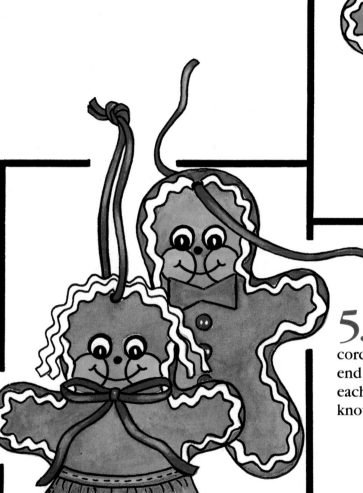

**5.** For the hanger loops, cut the rattail cord into two 8-inch lengths. Insert the end of one length through the hole on each ornament. Using the two ends, tie a knot in each length.

# stamped gift bag

## materials

Christmas card (old or new) with
"Merry Christmas" or other
holiday greeting

White bakery bag ($3^3/_4 \times 5^1/_2$-inch base,
11-inch height)

Holiday rubber stamps

Red or green ink pad (or any color to
coordinate with card)

24-inch length of red rattail cord

$^5/_8$-inch jingle bells: one red, one green

Two sheets of tissue paper (any color
to coordinate with card and
stamping ink)

## instructions

**1.** Carefully cut out a message from a Christmas greeting card, leaving between $^1/_8$- and $^1/_4$-inch trim around the outside edge of the letters. Plan where you are going to place the message on the bakery bag, but do not glue it on yet.

34

**2.** One at a time, gently press the rubber stamps onto the ink pad. Remove and press them onto the typing paper to practice stamping. Use a damp paper towel to clean the rubber stamps before changing colors and when you are finished. On the flat bag, stamp the designs on the area around where the message will be located. Glue the message onto the bag.

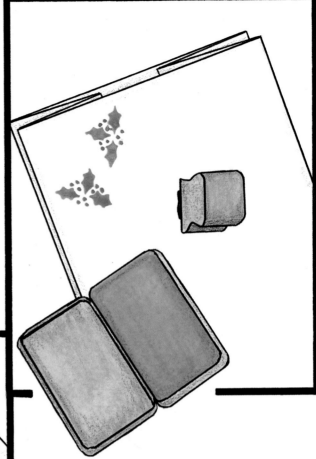

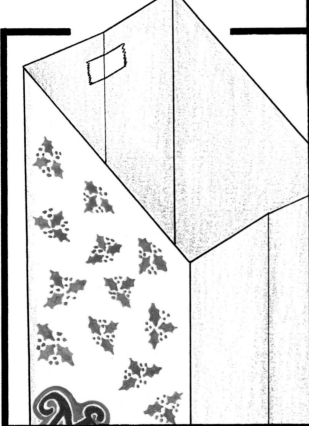

**3.** Before punching the holes for the handles, reinforce the area by placing a small piece of clear tape inside one of the narrow sides of the bag, centered and about $\frac{1}{2}$-inch down from top edge. Repeat this step on the other narrow side of the bag.

**4.** To make the handle, paper punch one hole through each piece of tape you just applied. Insert one end of the rattail cord through the inside of the bag and out the hole. Thread a jingle bell on the same end. Tie one knot on the end to hold the bell. Tie another knot about 2½ inches up through hole and around the top of the bag to keep the handle from slipping. Repeat to attach the cord to the other side.

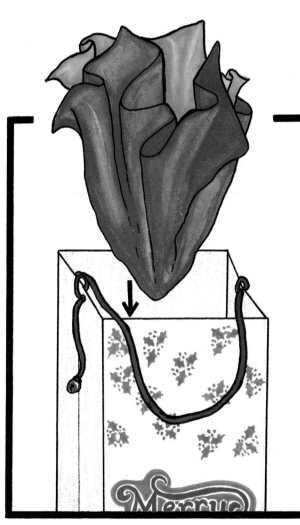

**5.** After placing your gift into the bag, you'll be ready to finish the project with this last step. To tuck the tissue paper into the bag, open each sheet and lay it flat on the work area. Layer the paper, making one sheet criss-cross over the other. Grasp the center of the pile and pull up to gather. (Be careful not to tear any of the tissue paper.) Push the gathers into the bag, and arrange the tissue paper at the top.

# felt tree ornament

## materials

Felt: 5 × 7 inches white,
  4½ × 5½ inches green,
  1 square inch brown
12-inch length gold sequin chain

½-inch gold or silver star gemstone
Sixteen 7mm assorted color gemstones
8-inch length of ⅛-inch wide red satin
  ribbon

## instructions

**1.** Using the patterns on page 60, trace and cut the background from the white felt; the tree from the green felt; and the trunk from the brown felt. Glue the trunk to the bottom of the background, leaving ¼ inch of the white felt showing around the sides and bottom. Glue the tree to the background, overlapping the trunk ¼ inch and leaving ¼ inch of the white felt showing around all sides.

**2.** To make the garland, glue one end of the gold sequin chain at the top left of the tree. Drape the chain back and forth across the tree, applying glue each time the chain changes direction. Glue the star gemstone to the background at the top of the tree. Finish decorating by randomly gluing gemstones to the tree.

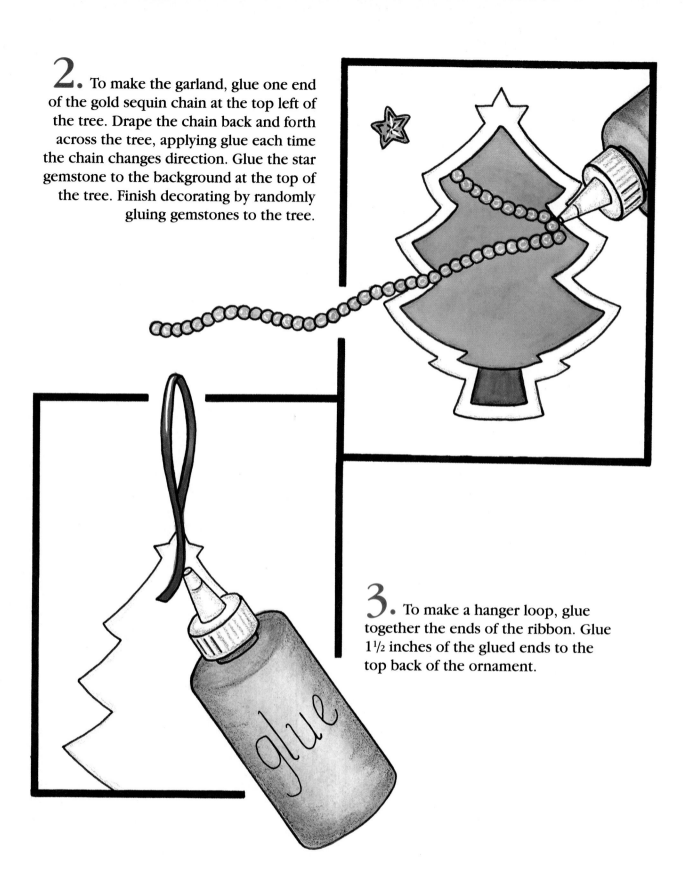

**3.** To make a hanger loop, glue together the ends of the ribbon. Glue 1½ inches of the glued ends to the top back of the ornament.

# elwood, the clothespin elf

## materials

Slotted round wooden clothespin
Red, green, and pink acrylic paint
Felt: 2 × 4 inches green, 1 × 2 inches
  white, 1 square inch beige

Twelve 5mm white poms
4-inch length beige chenille stem
Small amount brown mini curly hair
Black fine line felt tip marker

## instructions

**1.** Prepare a clothespin for painting by dividing it into areas with lightly drawn pencil lines. Make the first line ¹/₂ inch from the bottom for the shoes. Draw the second line ¹/₄ inch above the legs for the waist. Paint the bottom and top areas (leaving the head unpainted) with two coats of red; let dry. Paint the middle area with two coats of green; let dry.

41

**2.** Using the patterns on page 57, trace and cut the collar, hat, and buckle from the green felt and the belt from the white felt. Apply glue to the inside of the belt and wrap it around the waist. Apply a dot of glue to the center front of the belt, and position the buckle on the belt. Apply a dot of glue to each point on the collar. Position a pom on each point; let dry. Wrap the collar around the neck. Glue together the overlapping ends of the collar at the center back of the clothespin.

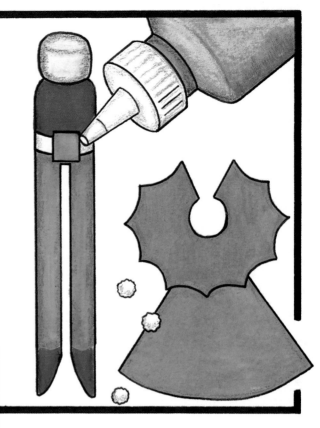

**3.** To make the hat, roll the green felt piece into a cone shape. Slightly overlap the straight sides and glue together. Fold over and glue the tip of hat. Apply glue to the point of the hat and position a pom at the point. Apply glue to the inside bottom of the hat and position it on the head.

**4.** For the toes, apply a dot of glue to the lower outside of each shoe and position a pom on each dot. To make one arm, cut a 2-inch length of chenille stem. For the hand, grasp one end of the chenille stem with the needle nose pliers, and coil 1 inch of the chenille stem. Apply glue to top of the straight end of the arm and position onto the side of the clothespin under the collar. Repeat to make and attach the other arm.

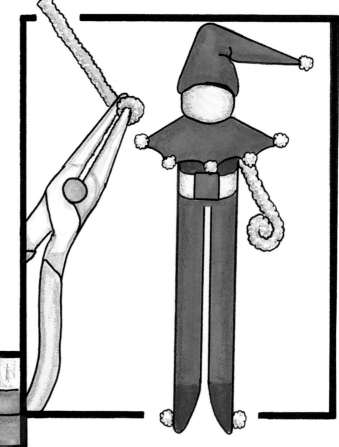

**5.** Using the pattern on page 57, trace and cut two ears from the beige felt. Apply glue to the straight edge of each ear. Attach one ear on each side of the head. For hair, apply a line of glue to the forehead from ear to ear and position curly hair on the glue. Paint two small pink circles for cheeks; let dry. Using the marker, draw the mouth, nose, and eyes.

# pine cone gift tree

## materials

Medium size old grocery box
Old newspapers
5-inch tall pine cone
Green spray paint
Red wrapping paper
Gift box (a 1½- to 2-inch cube)
Thirty 8mm red, white, and green
  beads

½-inch gold star gemstone
Small amount of gold metallic shred
12-inch length of 1-inch wide
  Christmas print ribbon
2-inch length white chenille stem

## instructions

**1.** In a well-ventilated area, cover the inside of the grocery box with newspapers. Place the pine cone inside the box. With adult help, spray the pine cone with two coats of green spray paint; let dry.

**2.** Wrap the gift box with the wrapping paper, using tape to securely hold it in place. Decide what side of the pine cone you like the best. Use this side as the front. Pick what side of the wrapped gift box you want to show in the front. Apply glue to the bottom of the pine cone and position it on top of the wrapped box so your two favorite sides are facing the same way.

**3.** One at a time, apply glue to the bottom of the beads, then place them on the ends of the pine cone quills. At the highest point on the pine cone, glue on the star. "Scrunch" the metallic shred. After applying glue around the base of the tree, arrange the metallic shred into the glue.

**4.** To make the bow, cut a 10-inch length of ribbon. Dividing the ribbon into thirds, fold the ends of the ribbon to the middle to form the bow. Position the middle of the 2-inch length of chenille stem at the front center of the bow. Wrap the ends of the stem around the back of the bow and twist together. Cut the remaining 2-inch length of the ribbon in half lengthwise. You will only be using one of the halves. Wrap the cut ribbon half around the chenille stem. Overlap the ends on the back of the bow and glue together. Glue the bow to the top front of the box.

# christmas card
# star

## materials

Christmas greeting cards (used or new)
8 × 16-inch white posterboard
Glittering gold dimensional paint

8-inch length of ⅛-inch wide green
satin ribbon

## instructions

**1.** Find designs and figures you like on old Christmas cards. The shapes can be irregular along the edges. They don't have to be exact because trimming will be done later. Cut out the shapes and set aside. Trace the star pattern on page 61 onto the posterboard two times. Cut out both stars.

**2.** Glue the Christmas card shapes to one star, overlapping card edges and allowing cards to extend beyond the star edges. Put your favorite picture in the center. (You should have a good number of card shapes leftover for the second star.) When the star is covered, trim the card shapes even with the star edges. Paper punch a hole near each point of the star. Leaving the center uncovered, repeat this step to cover the points of the other star.

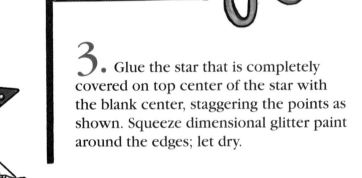

**3.** Glue the star that is completely covered on top center of the star with the blank center, staggering the points as shown. Squeeze dimensional glitter paint around the edges; let dry.

**4.** To make the hanger loop, insert one end of an 8-inch length of green satin ribbon through any hole. Bring the ends together and tie a knot. If you plan on hanging the star in a window, you may choose to decorate both sides (in Step 2).

# candy cane doorknob decoration

## materials

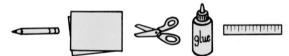

7 × 9-inch white posterboard
Felt: 7 × 9 inches white,
　1 × 12 inches red

18-inch length of ⅛-inch wide green
　satin ribbon
⅝-inch jingle bells: one each red,
　white, green

## instructions

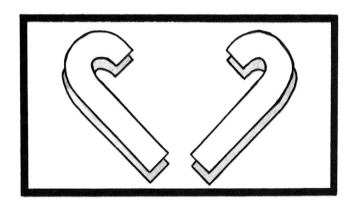

**1.** Using the pattern on page 63, trace and cut four candy canes—two from posterboard and two from white felt. Lay the posterboard canes on your work surface so the top curves face the center. Starting on the left side, glue the felt cane onto the posterboard cane. With the canes still facing each other, glue the other felt cane onto the right side.

**2.** To make the stripes, cut the red felt into two $\frac{1}{2} \times 12$-inch lengths. Cut each into four 2-inch lengths and one 4-inch length. Before gluing, place the stripes diagonally on the canes with the 4-inch lengths at the top curves. The ends of the stripes will overlap the edges of the canes. One at a time, glue the stripes onto the canes. After gluing, turn over each cane. Trim the excess red felt so the ends are even with the edges of the white felt.

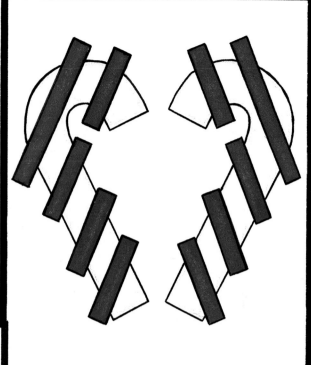

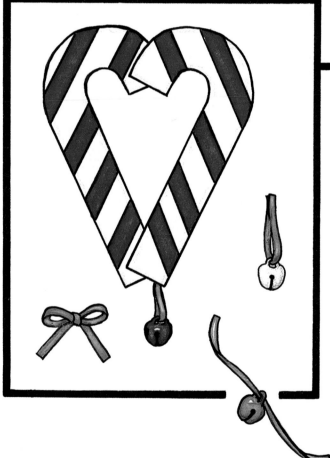

**3.** To assemble, overlap the canes at the top and bottom to form a heart shape. Glue the overlapping areas. Cut the ribbon so you have 3-, 4-, 5-, and 6-inch lengths. To attach the bells, insert one end of the 3-inch length of ribbon through the red bell loop. Bring the ends together and glue. Repeat using the 4-inch length of ribbon with the white bell and the 5-inch length of ribbon with the green bell. Glue ribbon ends to back bottom of the canes. Tie a bow in the remaining 6-inch length of ribbon, and glue it to the front bottom of the canes.

# christmas tree shirt

## materials

**Adult shirt:**
Felt: 8½×11 inches green,
  2½ square inches brown
34-inch length of ½-inch flat white lace
Twenty-six assorted color gemstones
One star gemstone

**Child shirt:**
Felt: 6×8 inches green,
  1½×2 inches brown
21-inch length of ½-inch flat white lace
Sixteen assorted color gemstones
One star gemstone

**For both:** White sweatshirt and repositional glue

## instructions

**1.** There are two patterns on page 64 for this project. Find the one that will fit the best on the size of shirt you want to make. Using the patterns, trace and cut the tree from the green felt and the trunk from the brown felt.

**2.** For the lace garland, use the glue gun to glue one end of the lace to the top left of the tree. Drape the lace back and forth across the tree, folding over and gluing each time it changes direction. When needed, add a spot of glue to any curves in order to keep the lace flat against the felt. Use the glue gun to randomly attach the gemstones to the tree. Glue the star gemstone at the top. Place the straight edge of the trunk under the bottom center of the tree, so that the tree overlaps the trunk by about ½ inch. Glue the trunk to the tree.

**3.** Turn the tree over and apply two or three coats of the repositional glue according to the manufacturer's instructions. Let it dry for 24 hours, then attach the tree to the front of the shirt. Remove the tree before washing the shirt.

elwood the clothespin elf                              soldier magnet

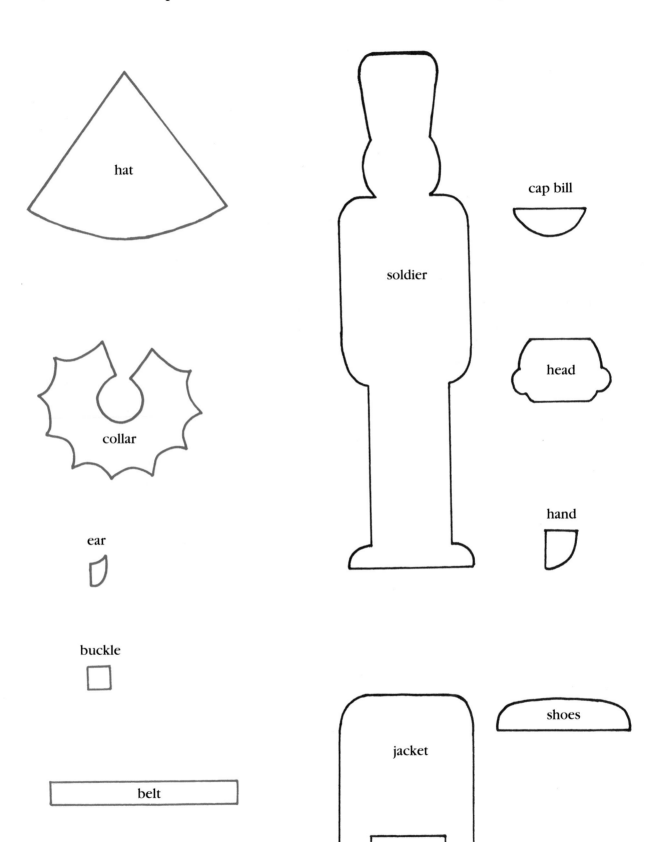

hat

cap bill

soldier

head

collar

hand

ear

buckle

shoes

jacket

belt

santa claus stocking

stocking foot

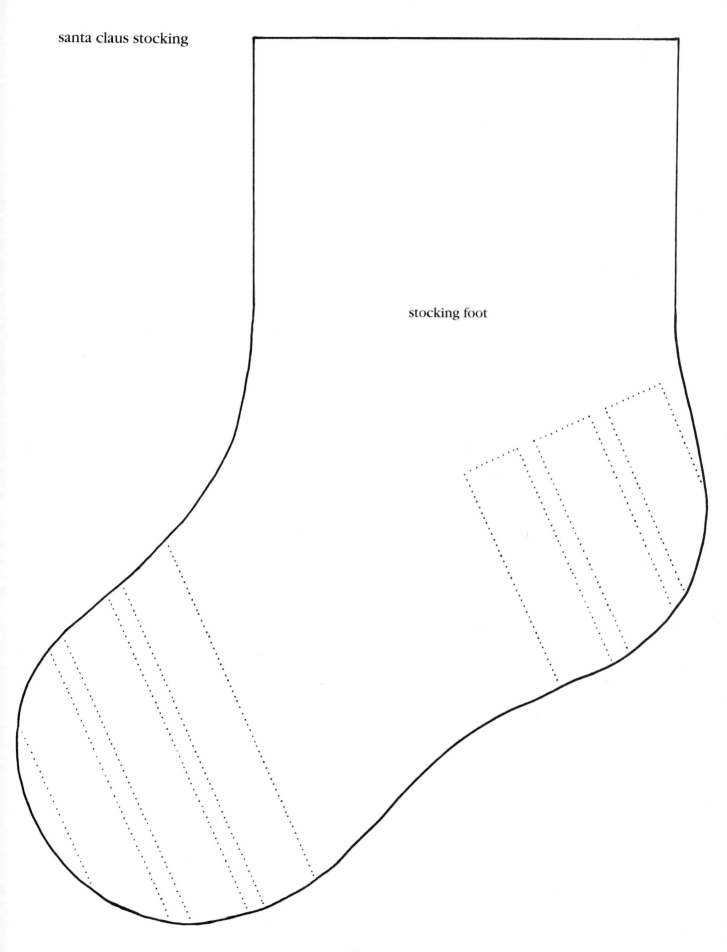

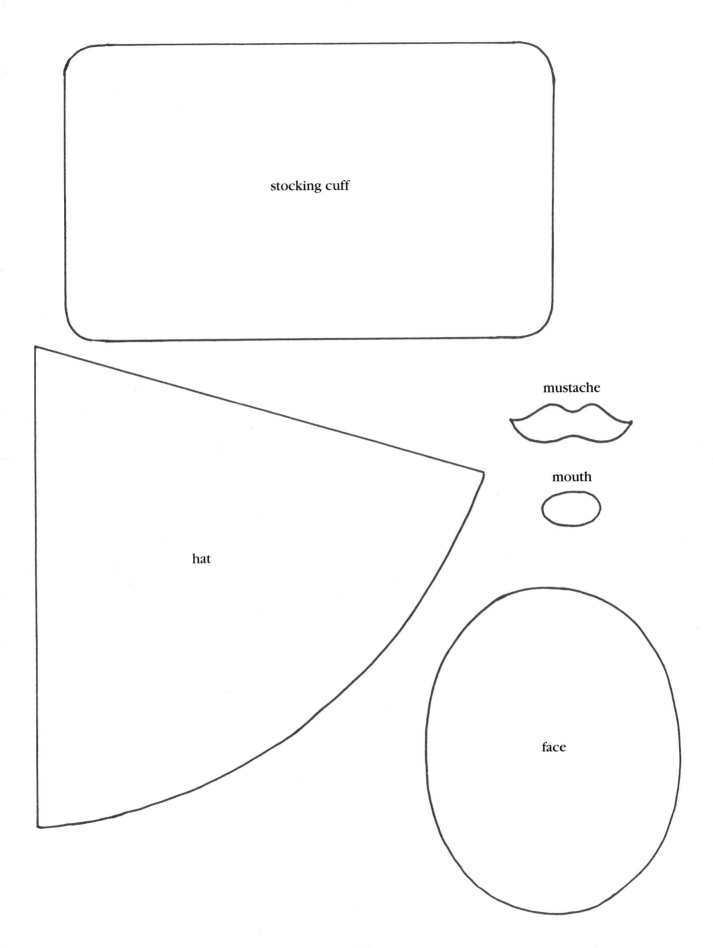

stocking cuff

mustache

mouth

hat

face

59

felt tree ornament

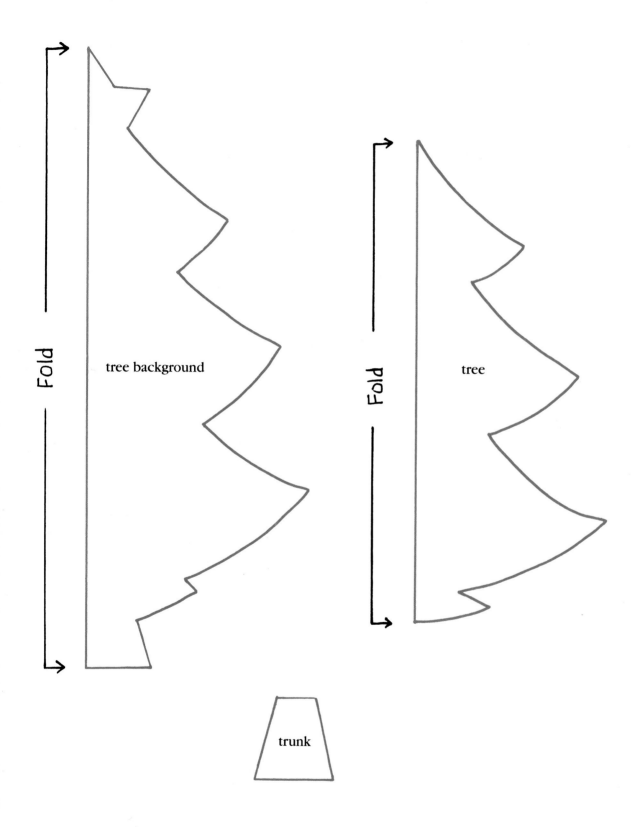

Fold

tree background

Fold

tree

trunk

"no worry" angel pin

mini-scene ornament

cheek

nose

wing

christmas card star

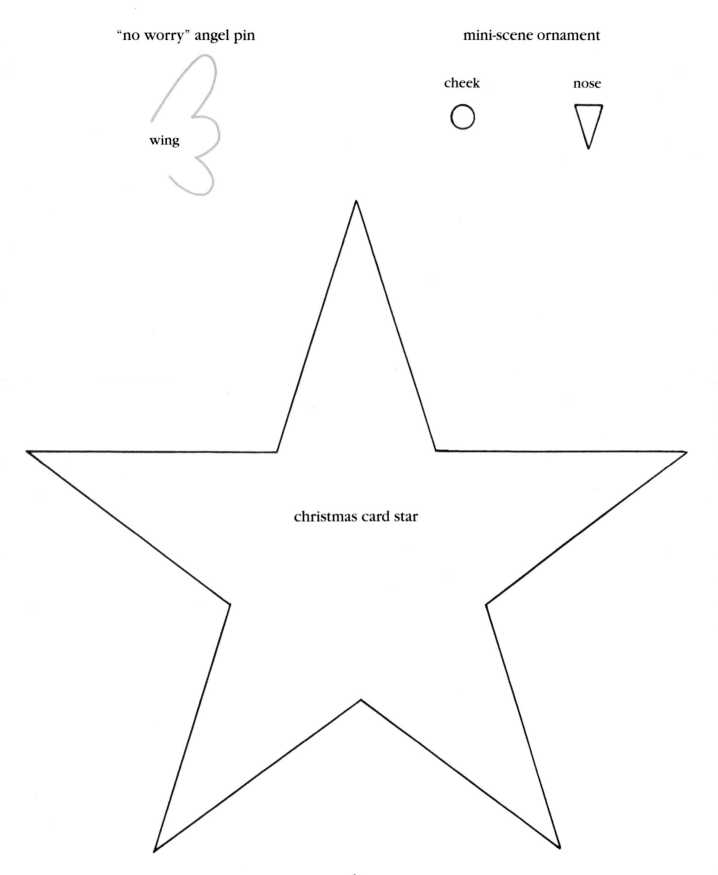

cross-stitch-look christmas card— grid pattern

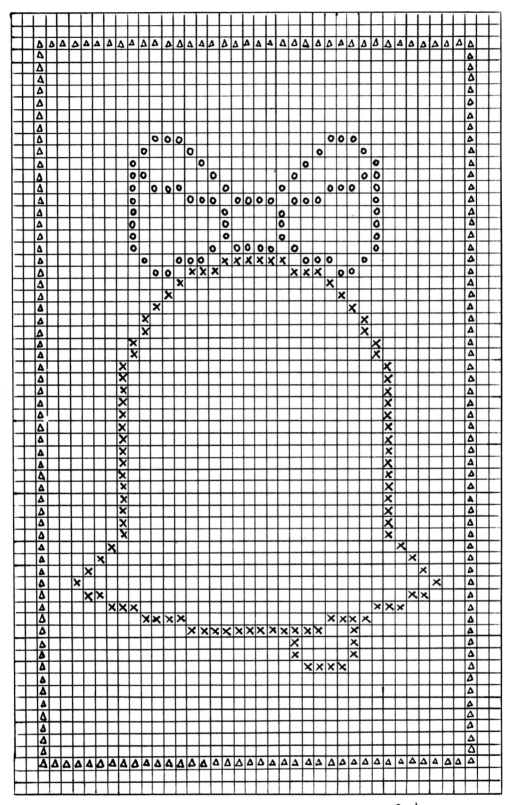

42 squares x 65 squares

o Red
x Gold
Δ Green

candy cane door knob decoration

gingerbread kid ornament

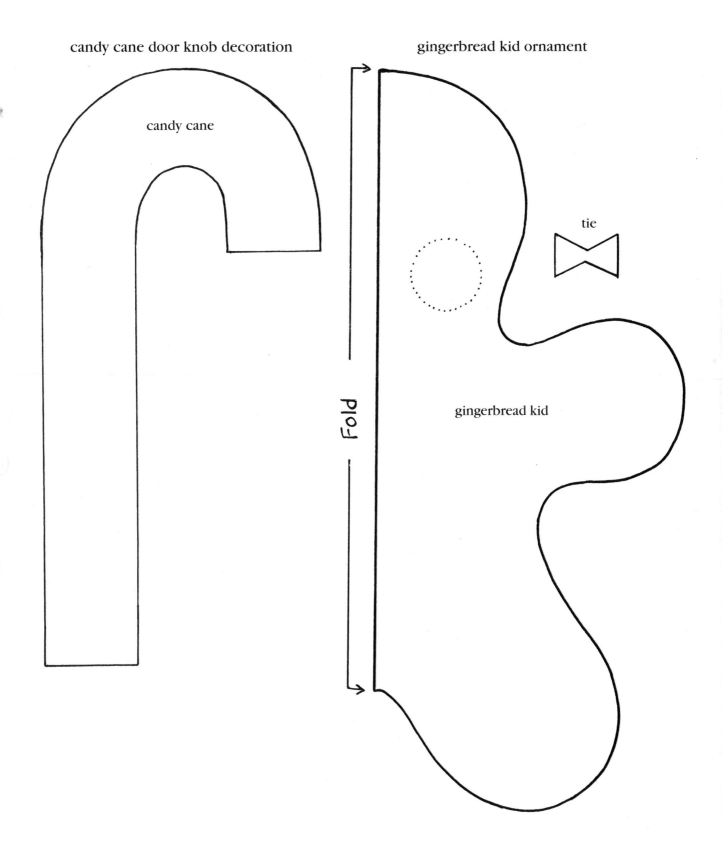

candy cane

tie

Fold

gingerbread kid

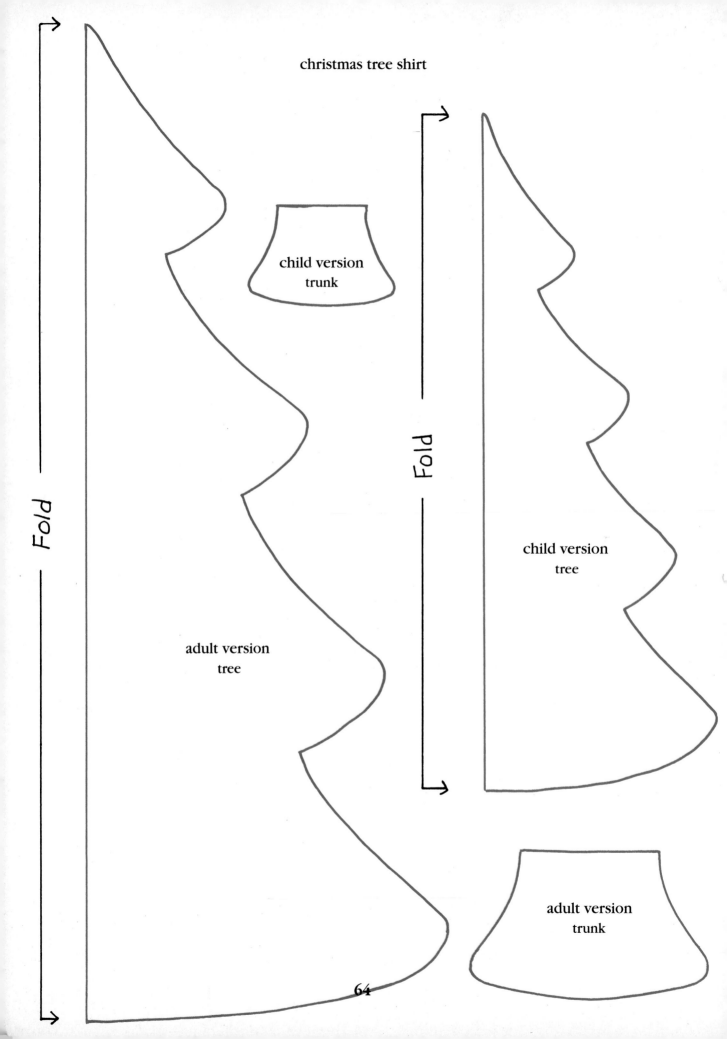

christmas tree shirt

child version
trunk

*Fold*

*Fold*

child version
tree

adult version
tree

adult version
trunk

64